Abstract

Extra value is calculated for 65 agricultural cooperatives by subtracting an interest charge on equity from net savings and also expressed as a percentage of operating capital. Cooperative performance is examined by type of agricultural cooperative—cotton, dairy, farm supply, fruit and vegetable, grain, sugar, and other—for 1992-96 and 2000-04. At least one cooperative of each type (except for sugar cooperatives) was able to show positive extra value when equity was assigned a charge 10 percent above the basic rate, while there were cooperatives of each type that showed negative extra value at the basic charge for member capital. Dairy cooperatives represented one-half of the top performers, while fruit and vegetable cooperatives represented one-half of those with negative extra value in both time periods. Results showed that cooperatives of all types can be very able performers but that some cooperatives may not be fully rewarding members for the use of their equity.

Key words: Extra value, extra-value index, cooperative, cotton, dairy, farm supply, fruit and vegetable, grain, sugar, performance.

Measuring the Performance of Agricultural Cooperatives

Carolyn Betts Liebrand
USDA Rural Development
Rural Business and Cooperative Programs

Research Report 213

December 2007

I0447029

Cover illustration from photo by Bruce Campbell

Preface

In response to inquiries concerning objective evaluation of the performance of cooperatives and cooperative management, an alternative method for cooperative members to evaluate cooperative performance was introduced in previous USDA Rural Development Cooperative Programs' research reports 166 and 212 and applied to dairy cooperatives. This extra value method was developed because the conventional measures of financial performance—return on equity, return on assets, return on operating capital, net margins on sales, net margins per unit, and so forth—do not yield unequivocal results. In addition, whereas the value of a company's stock may be used as a proxy for the company's performance and market value, cooperatives do not have stock exchange prices for an evaluation tool.

The previous reports calculated extra value indexes for dairy cooperatives and showed that this measure is an objective and definitive tool for comparing cooperative performance in creating value for member-producers. Therefore, this report extends the analysis by calculating the extra value index for agricultural cooperatives of all types. Only cooperatives that were on Cooperative Programs' "Top 100" list and for which there were sufficient data for the years considered were included. Sixty-five agricultural cooperatives met the criteria. The set of dairy cooperatives included in this study differs somewhat from the set of dairy cooperatives evaluated in Research Reports 166 and 212. Financial data for individual cooperatives are not disclosed.

The author wishes to recognize K. Charles Ling for his assistance in this project.

Contents

Highlights

The task of measuring the financial performance of cooperatives is made problematic by the attributes of the cooperative form of business. Most of the commonly used financial measures give an incomplete picture of a cooperative's performance. However, the extra value approach used in this report enables a cooperative's use of member-supplied funds to be fully measured—whether member capital is earning more, or less, than it could in alternative investments. The value a cooperative generates over and above its expenses, including an opportunity cost for its equity capital, is termed "extra value." A positive extra value indicates that a cooperative has created value by its operations, while a negative extra value means that a cooperative has actually diminished the value of members' investment.

Extra value is measured by subtracting an interest charge on equity capital from net savings. Three different interest rates are used for the charge on equity. The December average British Banker's Association's London Inter-Bank Offered Rate (Libor) plus 200 basis points provides the basic reference rate. This Libor + 2 "basic" rate represents the commonly held opinion that banks in the United States will generally extend loans to a firm with a better-than-average credit rating, at an interest rate of about 200 basis points above the Libor. Extra value was also calculated at two higher rates, the basic rate plus 5 percentage points and the basic rate plus 10 percentage points, to reflect a range of risk premiums because investors consider equity investment riskier than debt.

For comparisons over time and among different types of cooperatives, extra value is expressed as a percentage of operating capital. This common-sized index is thus scale- and operating mode-neutral.

Extra value was calculated for 65 cooperatives that had been on USDA's top 100 cooperatives (based on revenue) list for at least 4 years in each of two 5-year time periods—1992 through 1996 and 2000 through 2004. Looking at these two time periods allows for an examination of how cooperative performance progressed over time. Additionally, averaging over multiple years should have helped minimize the impact of extraordinary factors on results.

Performance was categorized into 5 groups according to the cooperatives' return on equity and extra value generated at the three different interest rates:

I—Negative returns. Cooperatives in this group had a negative average return on equity for the 5-year period.

II—Positive return on equity, but no extra value generated. These cooperatives averaged positive return on equity for the 5-year period, but showed a negative extra value when the basic rate was charged for equity capital.

III—Extra value generated at a basic interest charge for equity. These cooperatives were adding sufficient value through their operations to cover the opportunity cost of member-supplied capital at a rate similar to what they would have had to pay for debt capital.

IV—Extra value generated with a moderate risk premium on equity capital. Cooperatives in this group showed positive average extra value when interest on equity was charged at a 5-percent premium over the basic rate.

V—Extra value generated with a higher risk premium charge for equity.
Cooperatives in this category were able to average positive extra value for the 5-year period when applying a 10-percent risk premium (over the basic rate) to reflect the historic risk premium for equity investment.

More cooperatives showed positive extra value (category III, IV, or V) in the second time period (46 cooperatives) than in the first (39 cooperatives). The different types of cooperatives followed suit, with the exception of the farm supply cooperatives where there were two fewer cooperatives with positive extra value at any interest charge for equity in the second time period. For 2000-04, all of the cotton cooperatives showed positive extra value and over 80 percent of the grain and dairy cooperatives generated extra value. A majority of the other types of cooperatives generated positive extra value in the second time period.

Five cooperatives showed consistent and strong performance—generating extra value with a 10-percent risk premium added to the basic charge for equity capital in both time periods (category V). Three of these high-performers were dairy cooperatives.

Furthermore, except for farm supply cooperatives, cooperatives of each type were found in the highest performance categories—IV and V, in 2000-04. This indicates that a range of agricultural cooperatives is capable of performing admirably, regardless of the product they may handle.

On the other hand, with the exception of cotton cooperatives, at least one cooperative of each type failed to generate sufficient value to cover a basic charge for the use of their members' equity. However, fewer cooperatives of each type (except for farm supply cooperatives) lost value in the second time period as compared to the first. In fact, farm supply cooperatives were the only type where a majority dropped in performance category between 1992-96 and 2000-04.

The 65 cooperatives were ranked according to return on equity and by their extra value index at the three different interest charges. At the basic rate plus 10 percent rate, four of the 16 dairy cooperatives ranked in the top 10 in 2000-04. Just three cotton cooperatives were represented in the sample, two of which were in the top 10 in 2000-04. At the same time, a dairy cooperative showed the largest drop in rank between the two time periods among the 65 cooperatives and a cotton cooperative showed the second largest drop. Just one dairy cooperative was among the bottom 10 in rank—at the basic plus 10 percent rate.

Only two of the 9 farm supply cooperatives showed an improvement in rank between 1992-96 and 2000-04. Two other farm supply cooperatives ranked in the bottom 10, while none were in the top 10, for 2000-04 at the basic plus 10 percent rate.

The highest ranking and lowest ranking cooperatives were fruit or vegetable co-ops. At the same time, nearly three times as many fruit and vegetable cooperatives rose in rank as declined in rank between 1992-96 and 2000-04. In contrast, a majority of the other types of cooperatives fell in rank.

There was one grain cooperative in the top 10 for 2000-04, with two grain cooperatives ranking in the bottom 10. Sugar cooperatives were the only type not to have a cooperative in the top 10 in either time period. One of the other cooperatives (diversified, rice, poultry, or livestock) showed the largest rise in rank of the 65 study cooperatives, land-ing in the top 10 for Extra Value Index (EVI)—up from the bottom 10 in the first time period.

The results of this analysis show that at least one of each type of cooperative (with the exception of sugar cooperatives) in at least one of the two 5-year time periods considered, was able to add value sufficient to reward members for the use of their capital at a rate akin to the historic return to equity capital. Conversely, there were also cooperatives of every type that could not cover a basic charge for the use of member capital in at least one time period. Furthermore, for dairy, fruit and vegetable, and grain cooperatives, performances ranged from category I to category V.

The rankings allow cooperative performance to be judged relative to each other's performance. While all the cooperatives operated in the same general economic conditions of each time period, some saw their performance improve, while others' worsened between the two periods.

Several factors (such as a cooperative's pricing policies or the value of intangible cooperative benefits) are elusive to quantify and thus are not reflected in the various financial performance measures, including the extra value measure.

The exercise of measuring cooperative performance by the extra value method tells us that cooperatives of all types can be very able performers but that some cooperatives may not be fully rewarding members for the use of their equity.

Measuring the Performance of Agricultural Cooperatives

Carolyn Betts Liebrand
Rural Development
Rural Business-Cooperative Service / USDA

Introduction

The task of measuring the financial performance of cooperatives is made problematic by the nature of the cooperative form of business. In particular, many of the commonly used financial measures (return on equity, return on assets, net margins on sales, net margins per hundredweight of milk, and so forth) do not account for the cost of using members' equity in financing a cooperative's operations. Furthermore, cooperatives do not have a stock market valuation to offer a timely reflection of the value of the cooperative as a proxy for its performance (Ling 2006). As a result, members' ability to judge their cooperative's performance is incomplete. However, members need to be able to fully evaluate their cooperative's performance. The more complete the measure of cooperative performance, the better equipped the board is to guide the cooperative and to evaluate and reward cooperative managers.

The relative use of equity versus debt impacts the common performance measures in different ways. (This is illustrated in Table 1 where two hypothetical cooperatives are compared. Cooperatives A and B are assumed to be alike in every way—except for the degree to which they use member equity.) For example, two measures—net margins and return to equity—are impacted in opposite fashion by the relative use of debt and equity. A given cooperative with relatively higher use of debt will have higher interest expense and therefore lower net margins. At the same time, the relatively lower use of equity would result in a proportionately higher return on equity. In contrast, if the cooperative were to use relatively less debt and more equity, the reverse would be true.

Thus, one shortcoming of the financial performance measures frequently used is that equity is considered "free" capital by these ratios. But equity does indeed have a cost associated with it—it's just not one paid out with a line item on the operating statement. The cost is the potential earnings forgone by not making an alternative investment, known as the "opportunity cost" of making one investment over another. If members' capital was not committed to the cooperative, they could invest it elsewhere. The rate that members could realize in alternative investments is one way to reflect the cost of the cooperative's use of their capital.

A measure that takes into account the cost of member equity was introduced in USDA's Research Report 166 and further refined and simplified in Research Report 212. In both reports, this measure of cooperative performance—called extra value—was applied to evaluate dairy cooperative performance. This report extends the application of this extra value measure to all types of agricultural cooperatives.

Measuring Extra Value

The extra value approach used in this report follows the concepts embodied by the extra value measure developed by USDA Rural Development Cooperative Programs staff (Ling 1998 and 2006). Members can evaluate their cooperatives' use of member-supplied funds—whether their capital is earning more, or less, than it could in alternative investments. A positive extra value indicates that a cooperative has created value by its operations, while a negative extra value means that a cooperative has actually diminished the value of members' investment.

For the two cooperatives that hypothetically differ only in their relative use of debt and equity, Table 1 illustrates how they generate equal extra value, regardless of the way they were financed. While the common financial measures yield different results for Cooperatives A and B, the extra value these two cooperatives generate turns out to be identical. Thus these two cooperatives' operations each generated $32,000 in value above the cost of all their inputs, including a cost for using member capital.

Alternatively, if the appropriate charge for capital (both debt and equity) was higher, neither Cooperative A nor B created enough value to cover their total costs. Both cooperatives' operations decresed value by $18, 400.

While the sterile example in Table 1 serves its purpose in showing the strength of the extra value measure in theory, in reality, no two cooperatives are alike. To begin with, agricultural cooperatives vary dramatically in size and scope. Some market raw commodities, such as grain, while others provide producers supplies for the farming operations, and others provide both. Some are narrowly focused while others engage in a variety of enterprises. In addition, some may perform basic marketing functions while others engage in further processing, manufacturing, supply-

Table 1—Comparison of two cooperative using a variety of performance measures

	Cooperative A	Cooperative B	Comparison
Total assets	$1,000,000	$1,000,000	=
Operating Capital	560,000	560,000	=
—financed by debt	60,000	310,000	A<B
—financed by equity	500,000	250,000	A>B
Sales	5,000,000	5,000,000	=
COGS	4,500,000	4,500,000	=
Gross margin	500,000	500,000	=
Operating Cost	440,000	440,000	=
Operating margin	60,000	60,000	=
Cost of debt	5.0%	5.0%	=
Interest on debt	3,000	15,500	A<B
Net savings	**57,000**	**44,500**	**A>B**
Return on equity	11.4%	17.8%	A<B
Return on operating capital	10.2%	7.9%	A>B
Return on assets	5.7%	4.5%	A>B
Net margins on sales	1.1%	0.9%	A>B
Charge for equity	5.0%	5.0%	=
Interest on equity	25,000	12,500	A>B
Extra Value	**32,000**	**32,000**	**=**
Extra value index	**5.7%**	**5.7%**	**=**
Cost of debt	14.0%	14.0%	=
Interest on debt	8,400	43,400	A<B
Net savings	**51,600**	**16,600**	**A>B**
Return on equity	10.3%	6.6%	A>B
Return on operating capital	9.2%	3.0%	A>B
Return on assets	5.2%	1.7%	A>B
Net margins on sales	1.0%	0.3%	A>B
Charge for equity	14.0%	14.0%	=
Interest on equity	70,000	35,000	A>B
Extra Value	**(18,400)**	**(18,400)**	**=**
Extra value index	**-3.3%**	**-3.3%**	**=**

ing branded products to retail markets, and so forth. It goes without saying that the diverse nature of operations will require different levels of capital usage.

One way to neutralize the effect of this diversity of cooperative structures and operations is to express extra value as a ratio. Extra value divided by the cooperative's operating capital indicates the rate at which a cooperative is creating extra value. Operating capital represents the financial resources available to cooperative management to run the business.

Thus from our example, despite differences in capital structure (with all other things being equal), both Cooperative A and B created value at a rate of 5.7 percent when interest on debt and equity is 5.0 percent. However, if the appropriate interest charge for debt and equity is 14.0 percent, each cooperative's value is reduced at a rate of 3.3 cents per dollar of operating capital.

Extra value can be calculated from the information commonly found in cooperatives' financial statements. The only item that won't be found on standard financial statements is an interest charge for equity. Thus, the charge for equity capital must be assumed for calculating extra value. Furthermore, a representative interest rate paid by each cooperative for its debt capital may be difficult to arrive at due to the wide range of financing arrangements in and among cooperatives, depending on their particular situation with each creditor and/or debt instrument. However, for this extra value calculation, there is no need to determine a rate for the cost of debt capital since the cost of debt is reflected in operating expenses and subsequently, net savings. In this way, the extra value measure allows a cooperative's particular situation in debt markets to be preserved. Each cooperative may face a unique charge for its debt due to the nature of its operations, its past performance, and the particular arrangements it secures with available creditors, among other things. This method follows the revised calculation used by the creators of the value added measure in subsequent research (Davis 1993).

Additionally, for any interest-bearing equity, the charge paid out would also be reflected in expenses and thus this equity would not need to be included in the extra value calculations as "member equity."

The Extra Value calculations are as follows:

Extra Value = Net savings - Interest on Equity

Interest on equity	= member equity x interest rate for equity

Extra Value Index = Extra Value / Operating Capital x 100

Operating capital	= fixed assets + net working capital
Fixed assets	= non-current assets
Net working capital	= current assets minus current liabilities

Data

USDA annually publishes a summary of the financial performance of the 100 largest (based on gross sales) agricultural cooperatives. These are not necessarily the most profitable, just the largest in terms of sales. Agricultural cooperatives that had financial information in this USDA database for at least 4 years in each of the two 5-year time periods: 1992 through 1996 and 2000 through 2004, were included in this analysis (Table 2). Looking at these two time periods allows for an examination of how cooperative performance progressed over time. Cooperatives that were on the Top 100 list, but had data missing for more than one year in either of the 5-year periods were not included. Averaging over 5-year time periods (or 4 years in select cases: one cooperative in the first time period and 12 cooperatives in the second) should have helped to minimize the impact of extraordinary factors on results.

Table 3 shows how the study cooperatives in 2004 compared with the top 100 cooperatives of 2004. In numbers, they represented 65 percent of the top 100 cooperatives. Their combined total assets made up 60 percent of 2004's top 100 cooperatives' assets, while their net savings only came to 50 percent. Thus, the study cooperatives as a group had proportionately smaller total assets and net returns than the 100 top cooperatives. Furthermore, they appeared to be lower earners as a group, representing just 46 percent of the extra value generated by the top 100 in 2004 when a 5-percent interest charge is made for equity capital. (Note that the extra values in Table 3 reflect weighted-averages for the two groups of cooperatives.)

The cooperatives were grouped into 7 general types—cotton, dairy, farm supply, fruit and vegetable, grain, sugar, and "other" cooperatives, according to their main source of revenue. The few diversified (where both marketing and supply operations generate significant revenues) rice, poultry, and livestock

Table 2—Agricultural cooperatives included in the study

Cotton	3

Calcot, Ltd.
Plains Cotton Cooperative
Staple Cotton Cooperative

Dairy	16

Agri-Mark, Inc.
Alto Dairy Cooperative
Associated Milk Producers, Inc.
Cass-Clay Creamery
Dairylea Cooperative
DARIGOLD/Northwest Dairy Assoc.
First District Association
Md. & Va. M.P.
Michigan Milk Producers
O-AT-KA Milk Producers
Prairie Farms Dairy
St. Albans Cooperative
Swiss Valley Farms
Tillamook County Creamery
United Dairymen of Arizona
Upstate Milk Cooperative

Farm Supply	9

CF Industries, Inc.
Farm Service Cooperative
Fruit Growers Supply
Growmark, Inc.
Intermountain Farmers
MFA Incorporated
MFA Oil Company
Tennessee Farmer
Universal Cooperative

Fruit and Vegetables	15

Blue Diamoond Growers
Cherry Central Cooperative
Citrus World, Inc.
Diamond Walnut Growers
Knouse Foods Cooperative
National Grape Cooperative
Naturipe Berry Growers
Norpac Foods, Inc.
Ocean Spray Cranberry
Pacific Coast Producers
Saticoy Lemon Association
Sunkist Growers, Inc.
Sun-Maid Growers
Sunsweet Growers
Tree Top, Inc.

Grain	13

Ag Processing, Inc.
Aurora Cooperative
Champaign Landmark
Cooperative Elevator
Farmers Cooperative
Farmers Grain Terminal
Frenchman Valley
Harvest Land Cooperative
Heartland Cooperative
Pendleton Grain
Ray-Carroll Co.
South Dakota Wheat
West Central Coopertive

"Other"	6

Alabama Farmers (Diversified)
Equity Cooperative (Livestock)
Farmers' Rice Cooperative (Rice)
Gold Kist, Inc. (Diversified)
Land O'Lakes, Inc. (Diversified)
Producers Rice Mill (Rice)

Sugar	3

American Crystal
Minn-Dak Farmers
Southern Minnesota Beet Sugar

Total	65

Table 3—Extra value estimates for Top 100 cooperatives and study group of cooperatives, 2004

	Top 100	Study cooperatives[1]	Study cooperatives: Top 100	
	Number		*Share*	
Cooperatives	100	65	65%	
	Million dollars			
Total assets	25,104	15,143	60%	
Operating Capital	15,527	9,480	61%	
—financed by debt[2]	9,982	6,020	60%	
—financed by equity	5,545	3,460	62%	
				Diff.
Net savings	1,155	573	50%	(%-age points)
Return on equity	12.9%	10.4%		-2.5
Return on operating capital	7.4%	6.0%		-1.4
Imputed charge for equity	5.0%	5.0%		
Extra Value	878	400	46%	
Extra value index	5.7%	4.2%		-1.4
Imputed charge for equity	10%	10%		
Extra Value	601	227	38%	
Extra value index	3.9%	2.4%		-1.4
Imputed charge for equity	15%	15%		
Extra Value	323	54	17%	
Extra Value Index	2.1%	0.6%		-1.5

[1] Weighted average
[2] Includes minority interest in subsidiaries
SOURCE: Chesnick, USDA

cooperatives in the data set were combined in the "other" category. The fruit and vegetable group contains cooperatives that focus on a specific set of fruits or of vegetables. Farm supply cooperatives are organized to secure the inputs farmers need in their farming operations; however, many cooperatives whose main business is marketing a specific commodity also sell farming inputs to members. In particular, most grain marketing cooperatives also sell fertilizer, fuel, and/or offer agronomy services. Some dairy cooperatives, whose main line of business is marketing their members' milk, also sell dairy feed and other dairy and farming supplies, but these sales represent only a small portion of total sales.

The study cooperatives differed somewhat from the types of cooperatives on the top 100 cooperatives list in 2004. The study cooperatives had proportionate-ly fewer grain cooperatives than those on the top 100 list (20 percent versus 35 percent), and relatively more fruit and vegetable cooperatives (23 percent versus 14 percent). Keep in mind that the specific cooperatives on the top 100 list change from year to year, whereas the study cooperatives were the same set of cooperatives for all the years studied.

Interest Rates

Key to calculating extra value for each cooperative is the charge that has to be assigned for the use of member equity in cooperative operations. Theoretically, a charge equal to the interest rate a cooperative pays for its debt capital would represent an "opportunity cost" for the equity used by that cooperative (Ling 2006). In other words, if a cooperative doesn't use members' capital, it would have to pay another entity for capital with which to run the cooperative. Thus, the cost of member equity to the cooperative could be valued at what it would have to pay to secure the capital from another source.

Therefore, this report uses the same charge for capital that was used in previous applications of the extra value measure—the "Libor + 2." This rate is each year's December average British Banker's Association's London Inter-Bank Offered Rate (BBA Libor for U.S. dollar loans with a 12-month maturity) plus 200 basis points. Libor + 2 represents the commonly held opinion that banks in the United States generally will extend loans to a firm with a better-than-average credit rating, at an interest rate of about 200 basis points above the Libor (hence it is termed the "basic rate" in the following analysis). This rate is applied across all cooperatives on the member capital they use and is a consistent and simple way to account for the basic cost of member equity (see table 4 for the rates used).

But, the real question may be: What is the rate at which members would be comfortable investing their capital in the cooperative as opposed to some other investment? This is the opportunity cost to the member supplying the capital. It is commonly held that equity is riskier for the investor than debt is for lending institutions. Finance academics have noticed that, historically, the return to equity capital has averaged about 9 percent above the rate of return to debt-hold-

ers (Davis 1993). Other business analysts noted in the early 1990s that stockholders have received an average return that was six percentage points above long-term government bonds, noting that the rate was higher for more volatile stocks and lower for more stable stocks (Tully). Therefore, following the methodology presented in Research Report 212, extra value is calculated in this analysis at the basic rate, as well as basic rate plus 5 percent and basic rate plus 10 percent to indicate performance for a spectrum of risk levels.

All three rates reflect valid considerations of the cost of equity capital. The basic rate (LIBOR plus 2 percent) reflects the opportunity cost to the cooperative for using equity capital as opposed to debt capital. The "Basic + 5" and the "Basic +10" rates reflect two levels of members' risk premiums.

Results

Individual cooperative data cannot be revealed by USDA; thus, the results are presented in the form of performance category and rank among the group of cooperatives. The cooperative codes, do, however, reflect the nature of the cooperative operations. The cooperative codes beginning with "C" are cotton cooperatives, "D" = dairy cooperatives, "FS" = farm supply cooperatives, "FV" = fruit and vegetable cooperatives,

Table 4—British Banker's Association, London Inter-Bank Offered Rate (Libor), actual over 360-day basis; study interest charges on equity

Year	Libor, 12-month maturity, December average	Basic Rate (="Libor+2%")	Basic Rate +5% risk premium	Basic Rate + 10 risk premium
1992	4.1298	6.1	11.1	16.1
1993	3.7987	5.8	10.8	15.8
1994	7.5719	9.6	14.6	19.6
1995	5.5045	7.5	12.5	17.5
1996	5.7629	7.8	12.8	17.8
Simple average		7.4	12.4	17.4
2000	6.2374	8.2	13.2	18.2
2001	2.4167	4.4	9.4	14.4
2002	1.5773	3.6	8.6	13.6
2003	1.4960	3.5	8.5	13.5
2004	3.0151	5.0	10.0	15.0
Simple average		4.9	9.9	14.9

"G" = grain cooperatives, "OTH" = other types-consisting of diversified, rice, poultry and livestock cooperatives, and "S" = sugar cooperatives.

Performance categories—As in Research Report 212, performance was categorized into five groups according to the cooperatives' return on equity and extra value generated at the three different interest rates. Table 5 shows the number and types of cooperatives falling into each category for the two time periods.

I. Negative returns. Cooperatives in this group had a negative average return on equity for the 5-year period. In other words, their net margins averaged below $0, and it follows that the extra value measures also were negative. Four cooperatives (two sugar cooperatives, a dairy, and one "other" cooperative) fell into this category during the first period (1992-96). Five cooperatives (two fruit or vegetable cooperatives, one farm supply, and one grain cooperative) showed negative returns in the second period (2000-04).

II. Positive return on equity, but no extra value generated. In this case, the cooperatives averaged positive return on equity for the 5-year period. However, they did not generate value beyond the cost of the equity capital at the basic rate (LIBOR + 2 points), which means they showed a negative extra value. In theory, if they had borrowed the capital instead of relying on members to supply it, their net margins would have been negative. There were 22 cooperatives in the first time period and 14 in the second whose net margins were insufficient to cover a basic charge for the use of their members' capital. Only sugar cooperatives were not represented in the first time period, and only cotton cooperatives were not represented in the second. Farm supply and sugar cooperatives were the only types to show an increase in the number of cooperatives in this category from 1992-96 to 2000-04.

III. Extra value generated at a basic interest charge for equity. These cooperatives averaged positive extra value over the 5-year period, even after subtracting a basic charge for the use of member capital. These cooperatives were adding enough value through their operations such that they covered the opportunity cost of member-sup-

plied capital at a rate similar to what they would have had to pay for debt capital (LIBOR + 2). It goes without saying that the return on equity for these cooperatives (and for groups IV and V) was also positive. There were 19 cooperatives in category III in the first time period; while in 2000-04, nearly half-again as many, 28 cooperatives, were in this performance category. All types of cooperatives were represented in this category in each time period, with the exception of cotton cooperatives in the first period.

IV. Extra value generated with a moderate risk premium on equity capital. Cooperatives in this group showed positive average extra value when interest on equity was charged at a 5-percent premium over the basic rate. Members may not view investment in the cooperative the same as they would an alternative investment vehicle. Instead, they may accept a lower return on investment, in part as a cost of cooperative membership or, alternatively, as the value of having a cooperative with which to do business. Yet, since the risk associated with an equity investment is somewhat higher than a loan made by a lender, some sort of premium over the basic rate is warranted. The number of cooperatives in this group was similar between the two time periods—eight in the first and seven in the second. There weren't any cotton or "other" cooperatives in this group for either time period. Additionally, farm supply cooperatives were not represented for 2000-04. There were three dairy cooperatives, two grain cooperatives, and one fruit or vegetable cooperative in this category for each time period.

V. Extra value generated with a higher risk premium charge for equity. Cooperatives in this category were able to average positive extra value for the 5-year period when a 10-percent risk premium was added to the basic interest charge for equity. This is designed to reflect the opportunity cost to members for investing their capital in the cooperative rather than in an alternative investment (where the historic risk premium is thought to be around 9 percent). Twelve cooperatives were in this category in the first period, and nearly the same number, 11, in the more recent set of years. There were five dairy cooperatives, two cotton cooperatives, two fruit or vegetable cooperatives, one grain cooperative, and one "other" cooperative in this highest performing group for

Table 5—Performance of agricultural co-ops in the two 5-year periods, 1992-96 and 2000-04, by category

Group	Negative ROE	Positive ROE	Positive EVI @ Basic Rate	Positive EVI @ Basic +5%	Positive EVI @ Basic +10%	1992-96 average	2000-04 average
I	X					0 Cotton 1 Dairy 0 F. Supply 0 Fruit & Veg 0 Grain 1 Other 2 Sugar **4**	0 Cotton 1 Dairy 1 F. Supply 2 Fruit & Veg 1 Grain 0 Other 0 Sugar **5**
II		X				1 Cotton 4 Dairy 2 F. Supply 9 Fruit & Veg 4 Grain 2 Other 0 Sugar **22**	0 Cotton 2 Dairy 3 F. Supply 5 Fruit & Veg 1 Grain 2 Other 1 Sugar **14**
III		X	X			0 Cotton 4 Dairy 4 F. Supply 3 Fruit & Veg 5 Grain 2 Other 1 Sugar **19**	1 Cotton 5 Dairy 5 F. Supply 5 Fruit & Veg 8 Grain 3 Other 1 Sugar **28**
IV		X	X	X		0 Cotton 3 Dairy 2 F. Supply 1 Fruit & Veg 2 Grain 0 Other 0 Sugar **8**	0 Cotton 3 Dairy 0 F. Supply 1 Fruit & Veg 2 Grain 0 Other 1 Sugar **7**
V		X	X	X	X	2 Cotton 4 Dairy 1 F. Supply 2 Fruit & Veg 2 Grain 1 Other 0 Sugar **12**	2 Cotton 5 Dairy 0 F. Supply 2 Fruit & Veg 1 Grain 1 Other 0 Sugar **11**

2000-04. Dairy cooperatives were the only types to show an increase in the number of cooperatives in this category between 1992-96 and 2000-04.

Overall, more cooperatives showed positive extra value (category III, IV, or V) in the second time period (46 cooperatives) than in the first (39 cooperatives). The different types of cooperatives followed suit, with the exception of the farm supply cooperatives where there were two fewer cooperatives with positive extra value at any interest charge for equity in the second time period. For 2000-04, all of the cotton cooperatives showed positive extra value, and over 80 percent of the grain and dairy cooperatives generated extra value. And, a majority of the other types of cooperatives generated positive extra value in the second time period as well.

Table 6 shows the performance category of each cooperative for the two time periods and the change in performance category from the first period to the second, if any, for each cooperative. Five cooperatives showed consistent and strong performance—generating extra value with a 10-percent risk premium charged for equity capital in both time periods (category V). Three of these high performers were dairy cooperatives (D2, D10, and D11), while the others were a cotton cooperative (C6) and a fruit or vegetable cooperative (FV1). There were five more high performers—cooperatives that performed at performance level IV or better in both periods (D7, D9, G13, G15, and FV4).

Additionally, a cotton cooperative (C3) rose from category II to category V, while another cooperative (OTH5) rose from category I to category V! A grain cooperative (G8) improved two categories to category V for the second time period.

Five cooperatives improved their performance to category IV in 2000-04—three dairy (D12, D18, D14), a fruit or vegetable cooperative (FV17), and a sugar cooperative (S16). A grain cooperative (G15) maintained its performance in category IV for the two time periods, while another grain cooperative (G13) dropped from category V.

Thus in 2000-04, cooperatives of a variety of types were found in the highest performance categories-IV and V, with the exception of farm supply cooperatives. (However, one farm supply cooperative performed in category IV and one in category V in 1992-1997.) This indicates that a range of agricultural cooperatives is capable of performing admirably regardless of the product they may handle.

Cooperatives of every type were represented in performance category III for 2000—04, where nearly 40 percent of these were also in category III for 1992—96. Nearly equal numbers had improved to category III (nine cooperatives) as had declined to category III (eight cooperatives). There were more cooperatives in performance category III in 2000—04 than in 1992—96 for each type, except sugar cooperatives and "other" cooperatives, where there were the same number of cooperatives in both time periods.

Seven cooperatives maintained lackluster performance over the two time periods—not generating any extra value when a charge is imputed for member equity (category II). Over one-half of these were fruit or vegetable cooperatives (FV45, FV29, FV57, and FV60), while a dairy (D54), grain (G51), and another (OTH62) cooperative made up the rest. Six cooperatives dropped to category II in 2000—04. One-half of these were farm supply cooperatives (FS48, FS53, and FS58) while a dairy cooperative (D50), a fruit or vegetable cooperative (FV36), and another cooperative (OTH55) declined to category II.

One sugar cooperative improved from category I to II in 2000—04. The members of S49 may be somewhat encouraged by their cooperative's improvement from its negative average returns for 1992—96.

Finally, five cooperatives fell to category I for 2000—04. Two fruit or vegetable cooperatives (FV59 and FV65) along with a grain (G63) and farm supply (FS64) cooperative fell from category II, while a dairy cooperative (D61) fell from category III.

This shows that, with the exception of cotton cooperatives, at least one cooperative of each type failed to generate value sufficient to cover a charge for the use of their members' equity in either time period. However, with the exception of farm supply cooperatives, there were fewer cooperatives of each type that lost value in the second time period compared to the first.

Furthermore, members of the 12 cooperatives that either fell to category I in 2000—04 or stayed in category II for both time periods may be most concerned with their cooperative's performance. One-half of these lackluster performers were fruit or vegetable cooperatives (FV45, FV29, FV57, FV60, FV59, FV65), accompanied by two grain (G51, G63), two dairy (D54, D61), one farm supply (FS64), and one other cooperative (OTH62).

Rankings—Table 7 groups the cooperatives according to type and presents the performance categories and ranks according to EVI at the basic plus 10 percent rate

Table 6—Performance categories for individual cooperatives, 1992-96 and 2000-04

Coop Code	Performance Category 1992-96	Performance Category 2000-04	Change Period 1:2
FV1	V	V	=
D2	V	V	=
C6	V	V	=
D10	V	V	=
D11	V	V	=
FV4	IV	V	UP 1
D7	IV	V	UP 1
D9	IV	V	UP 1
G8	III	V	UP 2
C3	II	V	UP 3
OTH5	I	V	UP 4
G13	V	IV	D 1
G15	IV	IV	=
D12	III	IV	UP 1
D18	III	IV	UP 1
D14	II	IV	UP 2
FV17	II	IV	UP 2
S16	I	IV	UP 3
OTH19	V	III	D 2
FV23	V	III	D 2
FS26	V	III	D 2
G41	V	III	D 2
C52	V	III	D 2
G28	IV	III	D 1
FS34	IV	III	D 1
D37	IV	III	D 1
OTH20	III	III	=
FV21	III	III	=
FS24	III	III	=
G27	III	III	=
G32	III	III	=
FS33	III	III	=
S35	III	III	=
G38	III	III	=
G39	III	III	=
D42	III	III	=
FV47	III	III	=
OTH22	II	III	UP 1
G30	II	III	UP 1
FS46	II	III	UP 1
D25	II	III	UP 1
FV31	II	III	UP 1
D43	II	III	UP 1
FV44	II	III	UP 1
G56	II	III	UP 1
D40	I	III	UP 2

Coop Code	Performance Category 1992-96	Performance Category 2000-04	Change Period 1:2
D50	V	II	D 3
FS48	IV	II	D 2
FV36	III	II	D 1
FS53	III	II	D 1
OTH55	III	II	D 1
FS58	III	II	D 1
FV45	II	II	=
G51	II	II	=
FV29	II	II	=
D54	II	II	=
FV57	II	II	=
FV60	II	II	=
OTH62	II	II	=
S49	I	II	UP 1
D61	III	I	D 2
FV59	II	I	D 1
G63	II	I	D 1
FS64	II	I	D 1
FV65	II	I	D 1

for 2000-04, as well as the changes in these indices from 1992-96 for each cooperative. (Complete rankings according to return on equity and extra value at the different interest charges for both time periods can be found in appendix Table 1. The top 10 cooperatives according to EV1 at the basic plus 10 percent rate in 2000-04 are also in the top 10 according to return on equity (ROE) and EV1 at the basic plus 5 percent rate. Just one cooperative, D10, falls out of the top 10 and is replaced by D11 when ranked according to EV1 at the basic and the basic plus 5 percent rates. Four of these top 10 cooperatives—FV1, D2, C6, and D10, as well as D11, were also in the top 10 rank in 1992-96.)

The rankings allow cooperatives' performance to be judged relative to each other's performance. While all the cooperatives operated in the same general economic conditions of each time period, some saw their performance improve, while others' performance worsened between the two periods. Thus, cooperatives may want to assess the reasons their performance improved, or declined, relative to the performance of other agricultural cooperatives. Only four cooperatives ranked in the top 10 in both time periods; one half of these were dairy cooperatives (D2 and D10). Five cooperatives ranked in the bottom 10 in both time periods—three of which were fruit or vegetable cooperatives (FV57, FV59, and FV60).

Cotton cooperatives—Just three cotton cooperatives were represented in the sample, two of which were in the top 10 in 2000-04. While one cooperative dropped by just two positions to sixth position, the other two cooperatives showed wide swings in performance—C3 improved 48 positions to rank third, while C52 fell by 46 positions to rank 52 out of the 65 study cooperatives. These changes were the second largest increase and decrease in rank, respectively, among the 65 study cooperatives.

Dairy cooperatives—Four of the 16 dairy cooperatives ranked in the top 10. D2 was a consistent high performer—ranking second in 2000-04 and first in 1992-96. Two cooperatives (D7 and D9) improved 10 and nine positions, respectively, to land in the top 10. D14 showed the largest improvement in rank, improving 36 positions to 14 out of the 65 cooperatives. Meanwhile, D50 fell 47 positions to 50, the largest drop between the two time periods among the 65 cooperatives. Just one dairy cooperative, D61, was among the bottom 10 in rank.

Farm supply cooperatives—Just two of the nine farm supply cooperatives showed an improvement in rank between 1992-96 and 2000-04. FS24 improved 14 positions to 24, the highest rank held by a farm supply

cooperative, and FS46 improved 10 positions to 46. Two farm supply cooperatives ranked in the bottom 10 (FS58 and FS64). More than three-fourths of the farm supply cooperatives (78 percent) declined in rank—the highest proportion for any of the types of cooperatives. FS26 fell out of the top 10—from seventh in 1992-96 to 26th for 2000-04.

Fruit and vegetable cooperatives—Fruit and vegetable cooperatives showed the widest range in performance. FV1 improved one position to rank first in 2000-04, while FV65 fell 18 positions to last. FV4 improved 15 positions to fourth—the only other fruit or vegetable cooperative in the top 10. Four of the 15 fruit and vegetable cooperatives (27 percent) were in the bottom 10, where all but last place FV65 had improved their rank from 1992-96. More of the fruit and vegetable cooperatives had improved their rank (73 percent) than had declined in rank (27 percent). Moreover, proportionately fewer fruit or vegetable cooperatives declined in rank than among the other types of cooperatives.

Grain cooperatives—One grain cooperative (G8) improved 25 positions to eighth place while two grain cooperatives fell in rank to the bottom 10 (G56 and G63) for 2000-04. More than twice as many grain cooperatives fell in rank (69 percent) as improved in rank (31 percent) between the two time periods.

Sugar cooperatives—One of the three sugar cooperatives, S16, improved 36 spots to 16—the highest ranking sugar cooperative, while S35 fell nine slots to 35. The lowest ranking sugar cooperative (S49) had improved four positions. Sugar cooperatives were the only type not to have a cooperative in the top 10 in either time period.

Other cooperatives—One of the six other cooperatives (diversified, rice, poultry, and livestock), OTH5, showed the largest increase in rank of the 65 study cooperatives—rising 53 positions to fifth. Meanwhile, OTH19 dropped out of the top 10 to 19 for 2000-04, and OTH55 fell 24 positions to 55. OTH 62 remained in the bottom 10.

Group averages—The simple average of the individual cooperatives' performance is shown in Table 8. The 65 study cooperatives averaged positive extra value in both time periods at the basic plus 5 percent rate, a category IV performance. In other words, on average, the cooperatives had positive net margins after subtracting a moderate charge for the opportunity cost of equity. For 2000-04, this group of agricultural cooperatives created 2.3 cents in extra value for every dollar of operating capital expended, on average,

Table 7—Cooperative performance category and ranking 2000-04, with changes from 1992-96

Coop Code	Performance Category 2000-04	Change Period 1:2	Rank at EVI Basic + 10% 2000-04	Change Period 1:2	Coop Code	Performance Category 2000-04	Change Period 1:2	Rank at EVI Basic +10% 2000-04	Change Period 1:2
C3	V	UP 3	3	48	FV29	II	=	29	1
C6	V	=	6	-2	FV31	III	UP 1	31	1
C52	III	D 2	52	-46	FV36	II	D 1	36	-12
D2	V	=	2	-1	FV44	III	UP 1	44	4
D7	V	UP 1	7	10	FV45	II	=	45	10
D9	V	UP 1	9	9	FV47	III	=	47	-7
D10	V	=	10	-5	FV57	II	=	57	2
D11	V	=	11	-1	FV59	I	D 1	59	5
D12	IV	UP 1	12	10	FV60	II	=	60	5
D14	IV	UP 2	14	36	FV65	I	D 1	65	-18
D18	IV	UP 1	18	23	G8	V	UP 2	8	25
D25	III	UP 1	25	20	G13	IV	D 1	13	-1
D37	III	D 1	37	-22	G15	IV	=	15	-1
D40	III	UP 2	40	23	G27	III	=	27	16
D42	III	=	42	-17	G28	III	D 1	28	-12
D43	III	UP 1	43	-8	G30	III	UP 1	30	14
D50	II	D 3	50	-47	G32	III	=	32	-9
D54	II	=	54	-8	G38	III	=	38	-2
D61	I	D 2	61	-19	G39	III	=	39	-12
FS24	III	=	24	14	G41	III	D 2	41	-32
FS26	III	D 2	26	-19	G51	II	=	51	11
FS33	III	=	33	-12	G56	III	UP 1	56	-7
FS34	III	D 1	34	-14	G63	I	D 1	63	-9
FS46	III	UP 1	46	10	OTH5	V	UP 4	5	53
FS48	II	D 2	48	-35	OTH19	III	D 2	19	-11
FS53	II	D 1	53	-25	OTH20	III	=	20	9
FS58	II	D 1	58	-21	OTH22	III	UP 1	22	17
FS64	I	D 1	64	-4	OTH55	II	D 1	55	-24
FV1	V	=	1	1	OTH62	II	=	62	-1
FV4	V	UP 1	4	15	S16	IV	UP 3	16	36
FV17	IV	UP 2	17	40	S35	III	=	35	-9
FV21	III	=	21	13	S49	II	UP 1	49	4
FV23	III	D 2	23	-12					

when a charge for equity capital with a 5-percent risk premium over the basic interest rate was applied. However, if members' risk premium was 10 percent, the 65 cooperatives fell short of being able to pay member-producers this premium by $0.01 for each dollar of operating capital utilized, on average.

Grouping the cooperatives according to the product (predominantly) handled showed a range of performance. Again, the results presented are the simple average of the individual cooperatives' performance. Cotton cooperatives outperformed the other types—generating positive extra value with a 10-point risk premium charged for equity (performance category V) in both time periods. Dairy cooperatives performed almost as well—but dropped to performance category IV for 2000-04, missing members' expectations by an average of just $0.008 per dollar of operating capital when equity was charged a 10-percent risk premium over the basic rate.

The other five types of cooperatives all performed at category III for 2000-04, averaging positive extra value when charged a basic rate for their use of equity capital. Grain cooperatives generated an average of $0.02 in extra value for each dollar of operating capital used after accounting for a basic charge for equity. Along with grain cooperatives, farm supply cooperatives and other cooperatives performed at the category III level in both time periods, while fruit and vegetable and sugar cooperatives had improved their average performance from category II in 1992-96.

(For the weighted average group results, see appendix Table 2. Suffice it to say that for the cooperatives in this study, the weighted average was lower than the simple average in both time periods. This indicates that for this set of cooperatives, one or more of the larger cooperatives performed less well than the group. For 2000-04 this held true within each group except for the fruit and vegetable cooperatives where the weighted average was above the simple average—indicating one or more large cooperatives added relatively more value than the group.)

Conclusions

There are likely a variety of reasons that cooperatives of one type may perform generally better or worse than another. The most obvious is that the market conditions for one particular commodity may differ from the market circumstances for another. The market for tree fruit is impacted by different factors than milk markets. Farm supply operations face different operational challenges than cotton marketing. Moreover, each agricultural commodity type is subject to its own unique set of competitive and institutional factors that may impact a cooperative's ability to create value. At the same time, even within a commodity type, the market environment may vary according to the geographic region or market segment in which the cooperative operates.

However, the results of this analysis show that at least one of each type of cooperative (with the exception of sugar cooperatives) in at least one of the two 5-year time periods considered, was able to add value sufficient to reward members for the use of their capital at a rate akin to the historic return-to-equity investments. Conversely, there were also cooperatives of every type that could not cover a basic charge for the use of member capital. Thus, it appears that the ability to generate, or lose, value is not exclusive to cooperatives of one type or another. In fact, for every type of cooperative where there were more than three cooperatives in the group, performances ranged from category I to category V. Furthermore, the range of perfor-

mance within each group indicated that factors other than the commodities handled also play a role in how well a cooperative performs.

That said, among the highest performers, dairy cooperatives represented one-half of the 10 cooperatives that performed in category IV or V in both time periods. On the other end of the performance spectrum, fruit and vegetable cooperatives represented one-half of the 12 cooperatives that performed in category I or II in both time periods. Furthermore, no farm supply cooperatives performed better than the category III level in 2000-04.

While the performance of fruit and vegetable cooperatives ranged from the highest-ranked cooperative to the lowest, a majority (73 percent) moved up in rank relative to the 65 study cooperatives between 1992-96 and 2000-04. In contrast, a majority of the cotton, dairy, farm supply, grain, and "other" cooperatives fell in rank. Moreover, farm supply cooperatives were the only type where a majority (two-thirds, in fact) of the cooperatives dropped in performance category between 1992-96 and 2000-04.

Beyond the external economic and market factors impacting cooperative performance, cooperatives' pricing policies—the prices a cooperative pays members for commodities/charges for farm inputs—impact the various measures of financial performance, including the extra value measure. The prices paid, or charged, by a cooperative directly impact the level of the cooperative's net margins. As net margins are influenced, so is the resulting extra value measure. For example, a marketing cooperative may pay members high prices or premiums for their production, which means their cost of goods sold will be an elevated amount, lowering net margins and extra value accordingly. On the other hand, some marketing cooperatives may pay relatively low prices enabling the cooperative to show larger net margins and extra value (appendix Table 3). In the same way, a farm supply cooperative's charges for its products and services may be relatively lower (or higher), lowering (or raising) the cooperative's income and impacting the cooperative's bottom line correspondingly. Thus, the relationship between profits and value to investor-owners (members) of a cooperative business may not be as clear-cut as for an investor-owned business. Both the strength of the cooperative to its members as users (price levels) and as investor-owners (extra value) must be taken into account.

To one degree or another, cooperatives offer valuable, and frequently intangible, benefits that cannot be expressed in terms of dollars and cents. Thus, these

Table 8—Performance of study cooperatives, simple averages by type of cooperative, 1992-96 and 2000-04

| | ROE | Extra Value Index | | | Performance category | Rank | Equity share of operating capital |
		BASIC RATE (LIBOR +2)	BASIC RATE +5	BASIC RATE +10			
1992-96 Averages							
All (65 cooperatives)	11.9%	4.0	0.3	(3.4)	IV		74.5%
Cotton (3 cooperatives)	18.3%	10.1	5.7	1.3	V	1	88.0%
Dairy (16 cooperatives)	17.0%	8.9	5.1	1.2	V	2	76.6%
Farm Supply (9 coops)	10.5%	2.4	(1.2)	(4.9)	III	4	73.2%
Fruit & Veg. (14 coops)	6.2%	(1.1)	(4.6)	(8.1)	II	6	69.7%
Grain (13 cooperatives)	10.7%	2.4	(1.6)	(5.6)	III	5	79.5%
Other (6 coops)	8.3%	0.6	(3.0)	(6.5)	III	3	70.4%
Sugar (3 cooperatives)	1.9%	(2.8)	(5.7)	(8.6)	II	7	58.5%
2000-04 Averages							
All (65 cooperatives)	12.2%	5.6	2.3	(1.0)	IV		66.7%
Cotton (3 cooperatives)	22.9%	15.5	11.3	7.1	V	1	83.2%
Dairy (16 cooperatives)	12.5%	6.6	2.9	(0.8)	IV	2	73.7%
Farm Supply (9 coops)	5.1%	0.1	(3.3)	(6.7)	III	7	67.9%
Fruit & Veg. (14 coops)	5.6%	0.5	(2.4)	(5.3)	III	6	58.7%
Grain (13 cooperatives)	8.1%	2.0	(1.5)	(5.0)	III	5	69.2%
Other (6 cooperatives)	9.3%	2.4	(0.4)	(3.2)	III	3	56.1%
Sugar (3 cooperatives)	6.2%	0.5	(2.0)	(4.6)	III	4	50.7%
Change							
All (65 cooperatives)	0.3	1.6	2.0	2.4	=		(7.8)
Cotton (3 cooperatives)	4.6	5.4	5.6	5.8	=	0	(4.8)
Dairy (16 cooperatives)	(4.5)	(2.3)	(2.2)	(2.0)	dn 1	0	(2.9)
Farm Supply (9 coops)	(5.4)	(2.3)	(2.1)	(1.8)	=	(3)	(5.3)
Fruit & Veg. (14 coops)	(0.6)	1.6	2.2	2.8	up 1	0	(11.0)
Grain (13 cooperatives)	(2.6)	(0.4)	0.1	0.6	=	0	(10.3)
Other (6 coops)	(1.0)	1.8	2.6	3.3	=	0	(14.3)
Sugar (3 cooperatives)	4.3	3.3	3.7	4.0	up 1	3	(7.8)

benefits are not reflected in the extra value measure. These benefits may include such things as: the guarantee of a market for the member's products, a reliable source of farming inputs, reduced price risk, farm and marketing services, representation in policy and regulatory matters, enhanced bargaining power, market coordination, and so forth (see Liebrand). Cooperatives incur expenses in providing these benefits, but don't generally directly assess members for them. In addition, some functions that cooperatives perform serve the broader market, benefiting members and nonmembers alike. However, only the members share in the cost of providing these market-wide functions.

Finally, one may wonder about the dozen study cooperatives that lost value at the basic rate in both time periods and yet remain ongoing concerns, as well as the 25 cooperatives that were able to generate extra value only with a minimal charge for equity in one or both time periods. Perhaps members of these low performers feel adequately compensated for the use of their equity capital through relatively higher pay prices/lower supply and service costs. Possibly, members of these cooperatives place sufficient value on the intangible benefits of cooperative membership—as well as things like their belief in the cooperative form of business, traditional loyalty to their cooperative, and so forth—that they accept a lower premium for the use of their equity. Alternatively, quite possibly the cooperatives and their members were unaware that the cost of their equity capital was not being covered. Several investor-owned companies that began to consider their full cost of capital also found they had been posting negative extra value for years, unbeknownst to their managers (Tully).

In conclusion, this exercise of measuring cooperative performance by the extra value method tells us that cooperatives of all types can be very able performers, while some cooperatives may not be fully rewarding members for the use of their equity.

References

Chesnick, David, "Largest 100 agricultural co-ops post strong margins in 2004," *Rural Cooperatives*, January/February 2006, USDA Rural Development.

Davis, Evan, Claire Gouzouli, Magnus Spence and Jonathan Star, Measuring the Performance of Banks, *Business Strategy Review*, Autumn 1993.

Liebrand, Carolyn and K. Charles Ling. Value of Cooperative Benefits to Southern Dairy Farmers. ACS Research Report No 99, Agricultural Cooperative Service, USDA, 1991.

Ling, Charles K., Measuring Performance of Dairy Cooperatives, RBS Research Report 212, Rural Business-Cooperative Service, USDA, June 2006.

Ling, Charles K. and Carolyn Liebrand, A New Approach to Measuring Dairy Cooperative Performance, RBS Research Report 166, Rural Business-Cooperative Service, USDA, September 1998.

Tully, Shawn, The Real Key to Creating Wealth, *Fortune*, September 20, 1993.

Appendix Tables

Appendix table 1—Performance categories and rank for individual cooperatives, 1992-96 average and 2000-04 average

Coop Code	Rankings—1992-96						Rankings—2000-04					
			Extra Value Index						Extra Value Index			
	EQ:OC[1]	ROE[2]	LIBOR +2 7.4%	BASIC RATE +5 12.4%	BASIC RATE +10 17.4%	Performance Category	EQ:OC[1]	ROE[2]	LIBOR +2 4.9%	BASIC RATE +5 9.9%	BASIC RATE +10 14.9%	Performance Category
C3	18	48	48	49	51	II	27	4	3	3	3	V
C6	1	4	4	4	4	V	9	6	4	6	6	V
C52	20	5	6	6	6	V	4	37	30	47	52	III
D2	2	1	1	1	1	V	3	2	2	2	2	V
D7	43	18	17	17	17	IV	35	7	9	8	7	V
D9	3	17	11	13	18	IV	1	9	7	7	9	V
D10	11	6	5	5	5	V	22	10	11	11	10	V
D11	9	10	8	9	10	V	2	11	8	10	11	V
D12	42	21	23	21	22	III	11	12	12	12	12	IV
D14	52	57	52	52	50	II	49	14	14	14	14	IV
D18	31	39	39	42	41	III	54	19	18	18	18	IV
D25	56	53	51	48	45	II	48	25	23	22	25	III
D37	59	16	18	18	15	IV	51	44	46	41	37	III
D40	36	64	65	65	63	I	18	24	26	33	40	III
D42	24	26	24	25	25	III	25	43	38	42	42	III
D43	51	38	40	39	35	II	31	42	43	46	43	III
D50	26	3	3	3	3	V	36	53	53	53	50	II
D54	16	45	46	47	46	II	13	49	50	52	54	II
D61	27	40	38	40	42	III	17	61	61	61	61	I
FS24	23	32	29	34	38	III	28	18	16	19	24	III
FS26	17	7	7	7	7	V	40	21	20	23	26	III
FS33	62	22	26	22	21	III	46	38	41	35	33	III
FS34	39	19	20	19	20	IV	37	33	35	34	34	III
FS46	32	54	55	56	56	II	23	39	40	45	46	III
FS48	22	13	12	12	13	IV	33	50	48	48	48	II
FS53	53	30	34	29	28	III	29	54	54	55	53	II
FS58	19	27	27	31	37	III	8	51	55	58	58	II

Appendix table 1 (continued)—Performance categories and rank for individual cooperatives, 1992-96 average and 2000-04 average

Coop Code	Rankings—1992-96 Extra Value Index						Rankings—2000-04 Extra Value Index					
	EQ:OC[1]	ROE[2]	LIBOR +2 7.4%	BASIC RATE +5 12.4%	BASIC RATE +10 17.4%	Performance Category	EQ:OC[1]	ROE[2]	LIBOR +2 4.9%	BASIC RATE +5 9.9%	BASIC RATE +10 14.9%	Performance Category
FS64	40	60	60	60	60	II	32	63	64	64	64	I
FV1	10	2	2	2	2	V	14	1	1	1	1	V
FV4	65	20	25	20	19	IV	62	3	6	4	4	V
FV17	38	58	59	59	57	II	42	17	15	16	17	IV
FV21	37	31	32	33	34	III	58	27	36	25	21	III
FV23	61	12	16	15	11	V	50	28	21	21	23	III
FV29	64	46	45	38	30	II	63	55	51	44	29	II
FV31	57	41	41	37	32	II	39	30	34	32	31	III
FV36	60	28	31	27	24	III	55	48	49	43	36	II
FV44	5	43	43	46	48	II	16	36	31	38	44	III
FV45	47	59	57	55	55	II	52	52	52	49	45	II
FV47	28	36	35	36	40	III	12	32	29	40	47	III
FV57	7	50	50	53	59	II	26	58	56	57	57	II
FV59	13	55	61	63	64	II	57	64	63	62	59	I
FV60	12	56	63	64	65	II	7	56	60	59	60	II
FV65	58	61	54	51	47	II	53	65	65	65	65	I
G8	33	33	30	32	33	III	38	8	10	9	8	V
G13	35	11	13	11	12	V	20	13	13	13	13	IV
G15	41	14	15	16	14	IV	65	16	25	17	15	IV
G27	21	37	37	41	43	III	24	22	19	26	27	III
G28	29	15	14	14	16	IV	30	23	22	28	28	III
G30	44	47	47	44	44	II	41	34	32	30	30	III
G32	30	24	21	23	23	III	34	26	27	29	32	III
G38	34	35	36	35	36	III	44	41	45	39	38	III
G39	6	23	19	24	27	III	19	29	24	31	39	III
G41	45	8	9	8	9	V	21	31	33	36	41	III
G51	8	51	53	62	62	II	15	46	47	50	51	II
G56	4	42	42	45	49	II	5	45	44	51	56	II
G63	14	49	49	50	54	II	10	62	62	63	63	I

Appendix table 1 (continued)—Performance categories and rank for individual cooperatives, 1992-96 average and 2000-04 average

| | Rankings—1992-96 | | | | | | Rankings—2000-04 | | | | | |
| | | Extra Value Index | | | | | | Extra Value Index | | | |
Coop Code	EQ:OC[1]	ROE[2]	LIBOR +2 7.4%	BASIC RATE +5 12.4%	BASIC RATE +10 17.4%	Performance Category	EQ:OC[1]	ROE[2]	LIBOR +2 4.9%	BASIC RATE +5 9.9%	BASIC RATE +10 14.9%	Performance Category
OTH5	46	63	62	61	58	I	43	5	5	5	5	V
OTH19	49	9	10	10	8	V	60	20	28	20	19	III
OTH20	15	25	22	26	29	III	64	35	37	24	20	III
OTH22	54	44	44	43	39	II	61	47	39	27	22	III
OTH55	48	34	33	30	31	III	47	59	58	56	55	II
OTH62	25	52	56	57	61	II	6	57	59	60	62	II
S16	55	62	58	54	52	I	59	15	17	15	16	IV
S35	50	29	28	28	26	III	45	40	42	37	35	III
S49	63	65	64	58	53	I	56	60	57	54	49	II

[1] EQ:OC = Equity:Operating Capital
[2] ROE = Return on equity

Appendix Table 2—Performance of study cooperatives, simple averages by type of cooperative, 1992-96 and 2000-04

		Extra Value Index					Equity share of operating capital
	ROE	BASIC RATE (LIBOR +2)	BASIC RATE +5	BASIC RATE +10	Perf. category	Rank	
1992-96 Averages							
All (65 cooperatives)	9.6%	1.5	(1.9)	(5.3)	III		67.9%
Cotton (3 cooperatives)	20.8%	11.4	7.1	2.9	V	1	84.7%
Dairy (16 cooperatives)	11.5%	3.1	(0.6)	(4.3)	III	4	73.5%
Farm Supply (9 coops)	4.6%	(1.9)	(5.5)	(9.1)	II	6	71.6%
Fruit & Veg. (15 coops)	7.7%	0.3	(2.9)	(6.0)	III	5	63.0%
Grain (13 cooperatives)	16.4%	6.5	2.9	(0.8)	IV	2	72.3%
Other (6 cooperatives)	13.2%	3.7	0.5	(2.7)	IV	3	63.8%
Sugar (3 cooperatives)	-0.2%	(4.1)	(6.8)	(9.6)	I	7	55.0%
2000-04 Averages							
All (65 cooperatives)	7.4%	1.4	(1.5)	(4.4)	III		58.2%
Cotton (3 cooperatives)	17.2%	11.0	6.7	2.4	V	1	85.6%
Dairy (16 cooperatives)	12.0%	5.4	1.5	(2.3)	IV	2	76.2%
Farm Supply (9 coops)	1.9%	(2.1)	(5.4)	(8.8)	II	7	67.5%
Fruit & Veg. (15 coops)	8.7%	2.1	(0.6)	(3.3)	III	4	54.3%
Grain (13 cooperatives)	7.5%	1.7	(1.7)	(5.1)	III	5	68.4%
Other (6 cooperatives)	8.4%	1.5	(0.7)	(2.9)	III	3	44.2%
Sugar (3 cooperatives)	3.6%	(0.7)	(3.2)	(5.6)	II	6	49.5%

Appendix table 3—Comparison of different cooperative pricing policies

	Cooperative pay price level		
	At prevailing market prices	Premium above prevailing market prices	Less than prevailing market prices
Total assets	$ 1,000,000	$ 1,000,000	$ 1,000,000
Operating capital	560,000	560,000	560,000
—financed by debt	60,000	60,000	60,000
—financed by equity	500,000	500,000	500,000
Sales	5,000,000	5,000,000	5,000,000
COGS	4,500,000	4,600,000	4,400,000
Gross margin	500,000	400,000	600,000
Operating cost	440,000	440,000	440,000
Operating margin	60,000	(40,000)	160,000
Cost of debt	5.0%	5.0%	5.0%
Interest on debt	$ 3,000	$ 3,000	$ 3,000
Net savings	57,000	(43,000)	157,000
Return on equity	11.4%	-8.6%	31.4%
Return on operating capital	10.2%	-7.7%	28.0%
Return on assets	5.7%	-4.3%	15.7%
Net margins on sales	1.1%	-0.9%	3.1%
Charge for equity	5.0%	5.0%	5.0%
Interest on equity	$ 25,000	$ 25,000	$ 25,000
Extra Value	$ 32,000	$ (68,000)	$ 132,000
Extra value index	5.7%	-12.1%	23.6%
Producer impact	$ 0	$ 100,000	$ (100,000)